ONCE UPON A TIME...

...On the faraway world of Eternia, twins were born to the king and queen. But soon after their birth, the little brother and sister were separated by fate.

The boy, Prince Adam, grew up on the planet Eternia. There, he learned the secrets of Castle Grayskull and that he had a great destiny. Through a magical transformation, he became He-Man, the most powerful man in the universe, and he fought on the side of goodness.

His sister, Princess Adora, was kidnapped as a baby by the wicked Hordak. She was raised by him on the planet Etheria, a world that lived in misery under the rule of Hordak and his Horde.

Only after many years were Prince Adam and Princess Adora reunited. Like Prince Adam, Adora was given a magical weapon; hers was called the Sword of Protection. Adora's Sword of Protection gave her mighty powers. With it, she was transformed into She-Ra, the Princess of Power. Her beautiful horse Spirit became Swift Wind, a flying unicorn.

Adora stayed on Etheria to work on the side of the Rebellion, which was determined to return freedom to the land. This small but dedicated band was led by Angella, queen of the Kingdom of Bright Moon.

Adora guarded the secret of She-Ra carefully. Of her many friends, only the centuries-old Madame Razz and little Kowl knew who She-Ra, the Princess of Power, really was.

One other possessed the secret of She-Ra. High atop a mountain was the Crystal Castle, a shining palace that was She-Ra's special place. At the bottom of a mysterious pool in the castle dwelled the spirit of Light Hope, She-Ra's powerful friend.

No one but She-Ra could see this wonderful castle. And only on the day that all Etheria was free would Light Hope's secrets be known to all.

It was for that day, when goodness would reign again over Etheria, that She-Ra pledged her power.

The Spirit of She-Ra

Written by Bryce Knorr

Illustrated by Harry J. Quinn and James Holloway

Creative Direction by Jacquelyn A. Lloyd

Design Direction by Ralph E. Eckerstrom

A GOLDEN BOOK

Western Publishing Company, Inc.
Racine, Wisconsin 53404

Library of Congress Catalog Card Number 84-062815
ISBN 0-932631-09-6
A B C D E F G H I J

Classic™ Binding U.S. Patent #4,408,780
Patented in Canada 1984.
Patents in other countries issued or pending.
R. R. Donnelley and Sons Company

"Yes, Shadow Weaver," Hordak hissed. "Your plan might work. Come closer and tell me more."

Shadow Weaver whispered into Hordak's ear. The Horde leader licked his lips and smiled.

"I *must* catch Princess Adora," Hordak said. "I will not fail. This had better work, Shadow Weaver. Or else I will be chasing you next."

"Do not worry," Shadow Weaver said. "You will get Adora. And *I* won't leave you. I am not like Adora. I am not *good*."

"Don't say that word to me!" Hordak yelled. "Begin your spell. Show Etheria what happens to those who trick The Horde."

"Shadows of fear, flow through my fingers," Shadow Weaver said. "Find the one that Adora loves most."

"Follow me, Spirit," the shadowy horse said. Spirit trotted after the other horse. And Shadow Weaver jumped on Spirit's back.

"Easy, Spirit, easy," The Horde witch said. The shadows became a rope. She slipped it over Spirit's head.

"Don't be afraid. An old friend wants to see you. You remember. He is the one who gave you to Adora."

Spirit tried to run away. But the magic was too strong.

Inside Castle Bright Moon, Princess Adora woke up. She knew something was wrong.

"Spirit!" she cried.

Adora ran to the stable. It was empty. She found only one sign of her beloved horse. A single, silvery hair hung from Spirit's stall door.

"Spirit, Spirit," Adora cried. "Where are you?"

Her shouts woke up the rest of the castle. But Spirit did not come home. Everyone looked until the sun broke through the trees.

"Spirit didn't run away," Adora said. "I'm sure of it. Someone took her!"

"I'll help you!" Glimmer said. "We will get her back!"

"Thank you, Glimmer," Adora said. "Perhaps later you can help me. But Spirit is my horse, and I must begin the search by myself."

The others left. Kowl stayed behind.

"I know who you'll find first, Princess Adora," Kowl said. "A certain She-Ra, right?"

Adora drew her Sword of Protection. For the first time that day, she smiled.

"I wonder what Castle Grayskull's power would do to a Kowl," she joked. "Want to find out?"

"That's quite all right," the furry little animal said. He flapped away. "I have all the power I need."

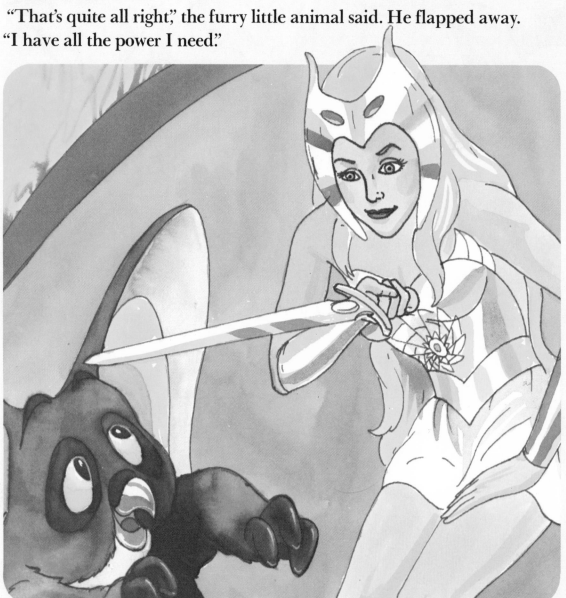

Adora raised her Sword of Protection. "By the honor of Grayskull," she cried.

"I AM SHE-RA!"

She-Ra ran through the woods. When the castle was out of sight, she whistled softly.

The treetops shook. Great wings beat the air. The graceful Enchanta landed gently beside her.

"I need your help, dear friend," She-Ra said. "Take me to the mountain. We must hurry!"

"Hang on," Enchanta said. "I need a good workout. We will be there before you know it!"

Enchanta flew to the bottom of the mountain. Fluffy clouds hid its rocky top. She-Ra climbed alone into the clouds. Above them, the sun shone proudly on her Crystal Castle.

Deep inside the castle was a dark pool. She dipped her Sword of Protection into the water. Its tip disappeared.

"Your eyes see all," She-Ra said. "Tell me where Spirit is. Please, I need your help, Light Hope."

She-Ra felt Light Hope's power. Two red eyes glowed at the very bottom of the mysterious pool.

"Do exactly as I say," Light Hope's deep voice said. "Go to the Forest of Fear. One who needs you will help you see."

"I don't understand," She-Ra said. "Whatever is my horse Spirit doing in the Forest of Fear?"

Light Hope's eyes grew dim. "Wait!" She-Ra said. But Light Hope said nothing and faded away.

She-Ra turned to go. "What's this?" she asked. By her feet was a golden collar. It was lined with red rubies.

"Oh, Light Hope," she said. "Sometimes you are so mysterious!"

Inside Hordak's jail, Spirit could not get away. Grizzlor came a little too close. Spirit pushed him with her head.

"I'll get you for that!" Grizzlor said.

"Stop it!" Hordak yelled. "Don't hurt the horse. At least, not until we have the Princess Adora."

Mantenna's eyes popped up. "Strangers are near the Forest of Fear," the lookout said. "But too much good is around them. My x-ray eyes can't tell who they are."

"It *must* be Adora," Hordak said. "My plan is working. Her love for that horse will be her downfall!"

The Forest of Fear was a thick woods. It dared anyone to enter.
"There is no path," She-Ra said. "I must cut my own." She took out her
Sword of Protection. It cut through the bushes.

She-Ra heard loud noises behind her. A growling wolf chased Kowl
down her path. Suddenly, Kowl flew into the air. He hung by his ears from
a rope. It was a trap!

"Yeeps!" he said. "Am I glad to see you, She-Ra! Everything's turning
around. Tell this overgrown mutt that I'm not his dinner!"

She-Ra took a running start. She grabbed the rope and swung over the surprised wolf. She and Kowl landed safely in a tree.

"Don't hurt my friend!" She-Ra said. She jumped down in front of the wolf. The animal hid its face in fear.

"Why, I didn't mean to scare you," She-Ra said gently. "You are nothing but a big puppy. Don't be afraid."

She felt something warm inside her cape. It was Light Hope's collar. She took it out. Its rubies glowed.

"Now, that's what I call a collar!" Kowl said. "But it's too big for me. Where did you get it?"

She-Ra told him Light Hope's riddle. "'One who needs you will help you see.' Light Hope told me that. Then I found the collar."

She-Ra looked at the wolf. "I wonder," she said. "It's worth a try."

She-Ra put the collar on the wolf. The rubies glowed as brightly as Light Hope's eyes. The wolf began to talk!

"I don't know how you can top that!" the wolf said. "Hey, I can talk!

"I'm sorry if I scared your friend. You see, I'm not brave at all. I thought I could act brave by scaring him."

Kowl flew down from the tree. He shook his fist at the wolf.

"Let that be a lesson to you!" he said.

"Wait 'til you try chasing someone again. It will be you who's caught in the trap!" Kowl said.

Kowl's angry words scared the wolf even more. She-Ra felt sorry for him. "Stop it, Kowl," she said. She-Ra picked Kowl up by his floppy ears. "The wolf said he's sorry. Scaring someone does not make you brave. You both know that now.

"What's your name, wolf?"

"Well, I . . ." the wolf began. "I don't have a name. I guess I never needed one before now."

"That's what you need, then," She-Ra said. "A brave name will make you feel braver. Let's see. You are gray. What about Graywolf for a name? Do you like it?"

Graywolf put his head back and howled. It was so loud, even Graywolf himself jumped.

"Oops!" Graywolf said. "I frightened myself. It's getting dark. This place is scary at night. I wish we had a light."

Graywolf's eyes began to glow!

"I don't know how you can top that!" he said. "We can look for your horse now. But the forest is a big place. Where do we start?"

Kowl snapped his fingers. "Of course!" he said. "Don't you get it? Gray-wolf is the one in need. He needs to be brave. His eyes will help us see."

Graywolf let his eyes shine on the woods. Silver hairs glowed in the light. They made a trail.

She-Ra gave Kowl a big hug. "You solved Light Hope's riddle. That's Spirit's hair! It leads toward the Fright Zone. Hordak took my horse!"

"Hordak!" Graywolf said in fear. Then he remembered his brave new name. He held his head high.

"Hop on my back," he said bravely. "And hang on! You too, Kowl."

Graywolf took them through the Forest of Fear. They finally reached the Fright Zone in the still of midnight. The trail of silvery hairs led to Hordak's hideout.

She-Ra heard a horse's cry.

"She must be there!" She-Ra said.

"I can't ask you to come any further," She-Ra said. "There is too much danger. Thank you both for your help. I could never have gotten this far without you."

Kowl was already crawling away. "Wait a minute," Graywolf said. He picked up Kowl in his mouth. "We have a job to do. I must prove I'm really brave."

"Oh, there you are," Kowl said. "I thought I'd lost you. L-L-Let's go."

The three friends carefully crawled to Hordak's tower. She-Ra found a door covered with cobwebs.

"Where are the guards?" Kowl whispered. "That's not like Hordak."

They walked up a flight of shaky stairs. They didn't see the silent alarms under their feet.

In the heart of the Fright Zone, bells rang.

"The trap is ready," Hordak said. "That alarm is music to my ears."

His men sharpened their weapons.

"Let's welcome Adora back home," Hordak said.

She-Ra reached the top of the stairs. She cried out in joy at the sight of her horse. Spirit was all right!

"You are glad to see me, too," she said. She-Ra combed her horse's mane while Spirit nuzzled her. Then she took out the Sword of Protection. Spirit became Swift Wind.

"No *way* you can top that!" Graywolf said. "But it looks like we have company."

Hordak ran up the stairs. He could not believe what he saw.

"She-Ra! What are you doing here?" he said. "That is not Adora's horse."

"Spirit is among friends," She-Ra said. "I wish I could say the same for you."

"Maybe I can't catch Adora," Hordak said. "But I think that you will do just as well, She-Ra."

Hordak pointed his ray blaster toward She-Ra.

"We must help her," Graywolf told Kowl. They jumped into action. Graywolf grabbed Hordak's sleeve. Kowl landed on Hordak's head and used his ears to cover Hordak's eyes.

Hordak fired. The ray missed She-Ra. It blew a big hole in the wall instead.

Graywolf held Hordak on the floor. None of The Horde could get past the brave wolf.

"Now's your chance, She-Ra," Graywolf said. "Get away while you can."

Hordak's blast had weakened the tower. It began to collapse around She-Ra and Swift Wind. She had only one choice. She grabbed little Kowl and jumped on Swift Wind. They flew into the sky as the floor fell in.

Hordak and Graywolf rolled across the floor. They both fell from the tower!

"Dive, Swift Wind," She-Ra said. But she could not reach them in time.

Hordak and Graywolf lay on the ground. They were stunned.

"I must help them both," She-Ra said.

She-Ra touched Hordak and Graywolf. A golden light circled all three.
Graywolf opened his eyes. "Boy, am I glad you topped that!" he
exclaimed.

"Hordak?" She-Ra asked. "Are you all right?" The Horde leader got up.

"Why did you help me?" he asked. "I am your enemy."

"My power is a great gift," She-Ra answered. "I must help whomever needs it. Maybe this will help you to become good."

"Good? Never!" Hordak yelled. He ran back to the Fright Zone.

"We had better get out of here, too," Swift Wind said. "I'll give you a lift, Graywolf."

They took off for the Forest of Fear.

Graywolf's fall made him forget She-Ra's secrets. But he remembered he was brave.

"Thank you so much," Graywolf said.

"Your bravery did not come from me," She-Ra said. "It was there within you all the time. I only helped you find it."

"I found it, too," Kowl said. "Hordak better not come around here again!"

She-Ra laughed. "There is more to bravery than that, Kowl. Sometimes the bravest thing you can do is be kind."

"That's right," Graywolf said. "I'm going to make the Forest of Fear into a Forest of Friends." Graywolf gave Kowl a big kiss.

"Well," Kowl said. "I don't know how you can top *that*!"

THE END

African American Life

Leaders
and
Movements

AFRICAN AMERICAN LIFE

LEADERS

AND

MOVEMENTS

by Hayward Farrar

Rourke Press, Inc.

The following sources are acknowledged and thanked for the use of their photographs in this work: Impact Visuals/Donna Binder p. 2; Envision/B. Wolfgang Hoffmann p. 7; Library of Congress pp. 9, 16; Janet M. Milhomme p. 11; Associated Publishers pp. 13, 18, 35; AP/ Wide World Photos pp. 21, 22, 25, 26, 31, 33, 37, 38; Lester Sloan p. 27; Odette Lupis p. 30; Frances M. Roberts pp. 40, 41.

Produced by Salem Press, Inc.

∞ The paper used in these volumes conforms to the American National Standard for Permanence of Paper for Printed Library Materials, Z39.48-1984.

Library of Congress Cataloging-in-Publication Data
Farrar, Hayward, 1949-
    Leaders and movements / by Hayward Farrar.
        p.   cm. — (African American life)
    Includes index.
    ISBN 1-57103-030-1
    1. Afro-Americans—Politics and government—Juvenile literature.
2. Afro-American leadership—History—Juvenile literature. I. Title.
II. Series: African American life (Vero Beach, Fla.)
E185.61.F197   1995
    324′.089′96073—dc20   95-10290
                                                                                            CIP
                                                                                            AC

First Printing

PRINTED IN THE UNITED STATES OF AMERICA

CONTENTS

Chapter 1

ROOTS OF AFRICAN AMERICAN POLITICS

American history would be very different without African American voters, politicians, and community leaders. Ever since African Americans began living their lives as free people, they have struggled for social, economic, and political equality in the United States. In 1865, the *Thirteenth Amendment* abolished slavery in the United States. In 1870, the Fifteenth Amendment made it illegal for states to deny anyone's right to vote because of "race, color, or condition of previous servitude." Without public support, these amendments to the Constitution were not enough to guarantee that African Americans would have political equality. The story of how African Americans found a political voice for their community in American government starts with the history of their ancestors in Africa.

Africa is the homeland of African Americans. In fact, it is the homeland of the human race. Ancestors of the first humans lived in Kenya millions of years ago. Africa was the home of the world's first organized society: Egypt.

ANCIENT EGYPT

The civilization of ancient Egypt is also known as *Kemet*. It began 5,000 years ago in the Nile River Valley. The Nile River is located in the northeast corner of Africa. This river provided the water and climate that Africans needed to plant crops. The river often flooded its banks, making the soil very rich and easy to farm. There was enough food for everybody. These conditions allowed Africans to build towns and cities and to create great kingdoms.

The rulers of Egypt were called pharaohs. The Egyptian people worshiped the pharaohs as gods who were all-powerful. The pharaohs' word, however, was law, and they punished anyone who disobeyed them. The Egyptian people were very loyal to their pharaohs and would do anything for them.

The pharaohs of Egypt ruled their country according to the principles of *ma'at*. These principles included truth, justice, righteousness, harmony, fairness, balance, and

Modern African Americans, like this young woman, enjoy equal access to the voting booth.

order. Every decision made by the pharaohs was measured against these principles.

The ancient Egyptians were builders. We can see this in their pyramids. After they died, pharaohs were buried in these huge structures. The biggest pyramid of all was the Great Pyramid, built for the pharaoh Cheops. This pyramid is almost 500 feet high. No one knows exactly how the Great Pyramid was built. The Egyptians must have had very good plans and tools to build such huge structures. The existence of the pyramids shows how important the pharaohs were to the Egyptian people.

The history of ancient Egypt is divided into different periods. During the period of the Old Kingdom, from 3200 to 2100 B.C., the Egyptians built the pyramids. The next period was the Middle Kingdom, beginning in 2100 B.C.. The Middle Kingdom ended in 1760 B.C., when people from Asia known as the Hyksos invaded Egypt. The Hyksos ruled Egypt for a short time. Then the Egyptian people drove out the Hyksos and established the New Kingdom, which lasted from 1700 to 525 B.C.

Ancient Egyptian civilization had its greatest accomplishments during this time. A woman named Hatshepsut was one of the pharaohs of Egypt during the New Kingdom. During Hatshepsut's reign, Egyptians sailed large ships into the Mediterranean Sea. They explored new lands and traded with the people there. Pharaoh Ahkenaton was famous for making his people worship only the sun god, Aton. This religion was one of the earliest examples of the worship of one god. Ahkenaton was married to Nefertiti. Her beauty is seen in murals and artifacts made when Ahkenaton was pharaoh.

In the period after 500 B.C., Egypt was invaded by the Greeks and the Romans. Foreign-born rulers controlled Egypt after that time. In later periods, the Arabs and the Turks controlled Egypt. Eventually, the British took control. It was not until 1954 that Egypt become an independent country again.

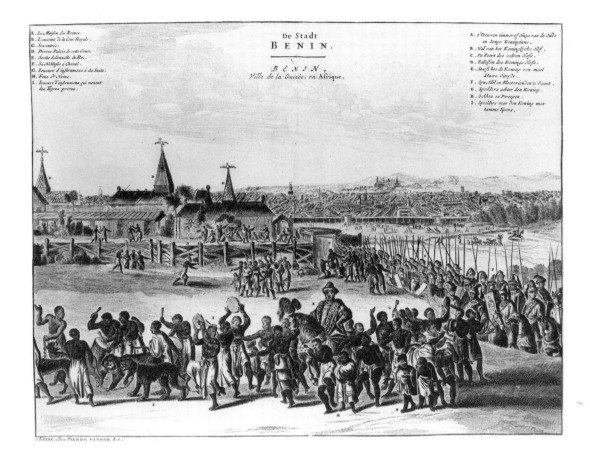

De Stadt
BENIN.

BENIN,
Ville de la Guinée, en Afrique.

Ancient African kingdoms flourished as independent political states long before Europeans colonized Africa in the nineteenth century.

THE GREAT WEST AFRICAN EMPIRES

The ancient Egyptians spread their civilization and culture to all parts of Africa. Their influence spread especially to West Africa. There great empires existed. Most African Americans were brought to America directly from West Africa.

Ghana. The first of these great African empires was Ghana. It existed from A.D. 700 to 1100. It was located in a great plains area called the *savannah*. The modern country of Ghana is named after this empire. People in the Ghanian empire were wealthy. The empire's wealth came from trading precious metals and woods, including gold and ebony. Traders from Ghana also traded ivory, precious gems, and other items to kingdoms throughout Africa and Europe. In addition, Ghana was a farming center. Farmers in Ghana raised wheat, sweet potatoes, and cattle. They used their land carefully because they did not have much rain to water their land. These farmers conserved other resources they needed to survive.

Ghana was ruled by emperors who were very much like the Egyptian pharaohs. They made and enforced the laws and were governed by the principles of *ma'at*. They had the love and loyalty of their people. People in Ghana paid taxes in cattle or other goods to their emperor. They also supplied him with soldiers to protect the kingdom. The most famous emperor of Ghana was Tenkamenin. He was known throughout Africa as a just and kind ruler.

The empire of Ghana fell after people from North Africa invaded. For a while after these invaders took over, there was little peace or order. Finally, a small kingdom called Mali conquered what was left of Ghana and created a new empire.

Mali. The Mali empire was even greater than the Ghana empire. Its founder was a powerful warrior named Sundiata Keita. He united smaller kingdoms in the area once ruled by Ghana. Sundiata was a fierce warrior who constantly defended his empire from invaders from the North. His successors took the Mali empire to new heights. It became one of the most advanced and powerful civilizations in the world. One of the Mali emperors actually went on a voyage across the Atlantic Ocean to the New World. The voyagers never returned to Mali. There are statues and coins found in South America showing African people. These people may have been the voyagers from Mali.

The most famous of the Mali emperors was Mansa Mūsā. Mansa Mūsā was a Muslim. He practiced the religion of Islam. The city of Mecca in Saudi Arabia is considered holy in this religion. To show their religious faith, all Muslims must visit Mecca. Mansa Mūsā's visit to Mecca was one of the most famous of all. Thousands of Malians went with Mansa Mūsā to Mecca. Mansa Mūsā also carried 40,000 pounds of gold with him. This gold would be worth hundreds of millions dollars today. He used this gold to pay for the building of roads, schools, hospitals, *mosques* (churches), and forts all through his empire. When he reached Mecca, he donated the rest to Muslim charities.

The Mali empire was made up of smaller kingdoms that paid taxes and supplied warriors to the Mali emperor. The Mali emperor held these kingdoms' royal princes and princesses hostage. He did this to make sure that these kingdoms stayed loyal to him. One of these hostages was a prince from the kingdom of Songhai. His name was Sonni Ali. He overthrew the Mali emperor and established the Songhai empire.

Drawing on traditions of the past, many African villages continue to rely on the political wisdom and guidance of tribal elders.

Songhai. The Songhai empire was the greatest of all the West African empires. The most famous emperor of Songhai was Askia Mohammed. He ruled Songhai from 1493 to 1529. Askia Mohammed created a well-organized and powerful empire. He did this by taking over the smaller kingdoms that made up the empire. He appointed governors to run these kingdoms as districts within his empire. These governors had to do what Askia Mohammed wanted. If any disobeyed, they could be severely punished. Askia Mohammed wanted to unite all of Africa under his rule. To do this he had himself appointed *caliph* of Africa. In the Arab kingdoms to the north, a caliph was the ruler of all Muslims. Askia Mohammed was put in charge of all Muslims in Africa.

The Songhai empire was very wealthy. Like earlier West African empires, it depended on farming and trade. People in Songhai sent gold, mahogany, ivory, slaves, and farm products north across the Sahara desert. They traded these products for cloth, salt, tools, and guns.

The people of Songhai lived in peace and harmony with each other. Family life was all-important. A person's identity came from his or her membership in a family. Even the emperors were not above or separate from their families. Riches were possessed by families. A family in Songhai shared everything. They shared the land, their houses, furniture, cattle, and other forms of wealth. Everyone worked together and shared the fruits of their work. Selfishness was almost unknown.

The Songhai empire began to fall apart after Askia Mohammed was overthrown by his son. The son was not as strong a leader as his father. He could not defend the empire from outside invaders. He also could not keep law and order. The Songhai empire broke up into many smaller kingdoms. If Askia Mohammed had succeeded in uniting Africa under his rule, its history would have been very different. This is because a united Africa would have been able to control the slave trade. Instead, European outsiders took over this trade. Because they transported so many

The slave trade threatened the stability of many African kingdoms.

Africans against their will, these outsiders began to destroy the stability of the African kingdoms. The slave trade eventually crippled Africa and the African people.

African empires had leaders who were strong and fair. When African people were brought to America to be slaves they continued to produce strong leaders who constantly fought for their freedom. These leaders followed the example of the pharaohs and the emperors of Ghana, Mali, and Songhai.

Chapter 2

AFRICAN AMERICAN POLITICS IN SLAVERY AND FREEDOM

From the 1400's to the 1800's, Africa lost millions of its people to the slave trade. European traders bought many people from African kingdoms and ethnic groups. Slave traders chained these Africans together and crowded them into ships sailing for North and South America. Because they were crowded together under unhealthy conditions, millions of these Africans died from diseases aboard slave ships. When the slave ships reached their destination, the remaining slaves were sold to slave owners living primarily in Brazil, the West Indies, and the American South. Many of these slave owners lived on large plantations where they forced their African slaves to grow sugar, coffee, rice, tobacco, and cotton. The Africans who were brought to the American colonies were the ancestors of modern African Americans.

AFRICAN AMERICAN RESISTANCE TO SLAVERY, 1700-1865

African Americans in slavery hated being enslaved. Even when they seemed to obey their owners, African Americans constantly resisted *slavery*. They made life hard for slave owners by not working very hard, breaking farm tools, burning down barns, making fun of their owners, and escaping from the plantation. Slave owners had to watch their slaves constantly to keep them from taking over the plantation.

Slave owners often punished their slaves to control them and make them behave. Many slaves hated the way their masters treated them and decided to take action. They met secretly to plan attacks on slave owners and their families. There were many slave revolts during the era of slavery. One of these revolts was led by Denmark Vesey.

Denmark Vesey was a slave who bought his way out of slavery. He became a rich carpenter in Charleston, South Carolina. He did not forget his fellow African Americans still in slavery. He plotted with many others to overthrow slave owners in Charleston. Vesey and his friends gathered weapons and recruited other slaves to be soldiers. They also tried to get money from Africans living on the island of Haiti. Vesey's revolt was planned for the second Sunday in July, 1822. Someone told the authorities about Denmark Vesey's plans. He and his friends were arrested, tried, and hanged. Denmark Vesey went to his death without revealing his plot.

Nat Turner led the most famous of all slave revolts. This revolt happened in Southampton County, Virginia, in 1831. Nat Turner was a slave preacher who received a command from God to free his people. During his revolt, many African Americans and white people were killed. The Army put down this revolt and arrested Nat Turner. He was tried and executed. These slave revolts put a great fear in the hearts of slave owners.

Free African Americans and white people who wanted to help began to work together to end slavery in the United States. Their activities were part of the antislavery movement.

Frederick Douglass and Harriet Tubman were two of the most famous African Americans who helped lead this movement.

FREDERICK DOUGLASS (1817-1895)

Frederick Douglass was the most important African American leader of the nineteenth century. He was born a slave in Maryland. In 1836, Douglass escaped to freedom in the North. He settled in Connecticut, where he became a ship builder. Then he became a leader of the antislavery movement. To help white people understand the horrors of slavery, Douglass published a book that told of his life as a slave. He also traveled around the country giving speeches. In these speeches, he called for the end of slavery. Next,

Frederick Douglass was one of the most outspoken critics of slavery in the United States.

Douglass started an antislavery newspaper called *The North Star*. He published this newspaper in Rochester, New York, which had become his home. During the Civil War, he recruited African American troops to fight in the Union Army. After the war, he served as a bank president and federal government official.

HARRIET TUBMAN (1820-1913)

Another important leader of the antislavery movement was Harriet Tubman. She was a runaway slave before she joined the Underground Railroad. The Underground Railroad was a group of people who went to the South to lead slaves to freedom. Harriet Tubman was known as a conductor in the Underground Railroad. In this role, she found slaves who wanted to run away from their plantations. Then she led them north to freedom. She was a very courageous person who risked death while she led slaves to freedom. She led more than three hundred slaves to freedom. During the Civil War, Tubman served as a spy for the Union Army. After the Civil War, she traveled around the country giving lectures about her experiences.

African American resistance to slavery helped the North win the Civil War. Many slaves deserted their plantations to join the Union Army. Others stayed behind to fight plantation owners. The Civil War brought an end to slavery. Through their participation in slave revolts, in the antislavery movement, and finally in the Civil War, African Americans helped bring an end to slavery.

AFRICAN AMERICANS IN FREEDOM, 1865-1900

After the Civil War, African Americans took advantage of their new freedom by starting families, going to school to get an education, and voting in elections. In the ten years following the end of the war, African Americans in the South elected black sheriffs, judges, state legislators, and representatives to *Congress*. One of these representatives was elected to serve as a senator. His name was Blanche K. Bruce.

Senator Blanche K. Bruce represented the state of Mississippi in Congress from 1875 until 1881.

BLANCHE K. BRUCE (1841-1898)

Blanche K. Bruce was the first African American elected to the United States *Senate*. He was born into slavery in Farmville, Virginia, in 1841. He moved with his owners to Missouri in 1851 and eventually received his freedom during the Civil War. In 1868, Bruce moved to Mississippi, where he became a landowner. Before becoming a U.S. Senator, he served in local government as a tax assessor and a county sheriff. In 1874, he was elected to represent the state of Mississippi in the Senate. While in the Senate, he spoke up for the rights of African Americans, Native Americans, and Asian Americans. He served in the Senate until 1880. After leaving the Senate, Bruce held several federal posts, mostly with the Treasury Department, until his death in 1898.

AFRICAN AMERICANS LOSE THEIR POLITICAL POWER

Former slave owners were frightened by the growing political influence of African Americans in the South. They feared that the former slaves would take over the South. To prevent this, the former slave owners tried to keep African Americans from voting. This took some time, but by the 1890's, these Southern whites were succeeding. New laws made voters prove they could read or write. These laws also made voters pay a tax before they could vote, called a *poll tax*. Finally, all those who wanted to vote had to own property. Many African Americans in the South could not read or write. Most of them were too poor to pay a poll tax or own lots of property. After these laws were passed, most African Americans could not vote. They could not elect any African Americans to hold political office. Only in the North were African Americans free to vote. The lack of voting rights caused many African Americans to move from the South to the North.

Chapter 3

AFRICAN AMERICAN POLITICS IN THE TWENTIETH CENTURY

During the twentieth century, millions of African Americans moved from the South to the North in search of jobs, educations, and the right to vote. They created large African American communities in Chicago, New York City, Philadelphia, Detroit, Boston, Baltimore, Los Angeles, Cleveland, and elsewhere. In these cities, African Americans voted for and elected black city council members, mayors, state legislators, and congressional representatives.

LOCAL POLITICS IN NORTHERN CITIES: CHICAGO AND NEW YORK

In 1917, African American voters helped elect Oscar De Priest to be the first African American on the Board of Aldermen (city council) in Chicago. Later, African Americans elected more African Americans to the Board of Aldermen. These black officials encouraged the city to hire more African American police officers, firefighters, and city workers.

African Americans also voted for African American delegates and senators to the Illinois state legislature. Eventually, many African Americans in Chicago became voters. Many of them wanted to see an African American candidate run for mayor of Chicago. In 1983, black voters elected Harold Washington to be Chicago's first African American mayor. He served as the city's mayor until his death in 1987. During the 1990's, African American voters in Chicago helped elect several black representatives to the Illinois state legislature and to Congress.

Many African Americans moved to New York City in the early twentieth century. There they elected African American city council members, judges, and state assembly representatives. As in Chicago, these New York state and city officials encouraged the hiring of many African American police officers, firefighters, and city workers. In 1989, David Dinkins became the first African American mayor of New York. He served until 1993, when he lost the mayor's election to Rudolph Giuliani.

David Dinkins was elected president of the Borough of Manhattan before he became the mayor of New York City in 1989.

AFRICAN AMERICAN MAYORS IN OTHER CITIES

Chicago and New York were not the only cities where African Americans were elected as mayors. For example, Carl Stokes served as the mayor of Cleveland from 1967 to 1971. W. Wilson Goode was elected to serve as the mayor of Philadelphia from 1984 to 1992. Kurt Schmoke was first elected as the mayor of Baltimore in 1987. All of these mayors gave thousands of African Americans city government jobs. Their example of leadership gave African Americans pride in themselves. One example of a great African American mayor is Thomas Bradley, who was elected as the first African American mayor of Los Angeles.

THOMAS BRADLEY (BORN 1917)

Thomas Bradley was born in 1917 in Texas and moved with his family to California after he was six years old. He attended the University of California at Los Angeles (UCLA)

As mayor of Los Angeles, Tom Bradley served for twenty years before deciding not to run for a sixth term.

before entering the police academy in 1940. Bradley worked as a police officer for many years and earned his law degree before retiring from the police force in 1961. He was elected in 1963 to serve on the Los Angeles city council. In 1973, Bradley was elected as mayor of Los Angeles. He served for five terms before retiring from office in 1993. While Bradley was mayor, Los Angeles rebuilt its downtown and expanded its airport. He ran for office as governor of California twice but lost each time. As a result of his leadership in Los Angeles, Bradley became one of the most respected politicians in America.

AFRICAN AMERICANS ELECTED TO CONGRESS FROM THE NORTH

African Americans in Chicago and New York City have elected many black representatives to Congress. The first were Oscar De Priest from Chicago and Adam Clayton Powell, Jr., and Shirley Chisholm from New York.

OSCAR DE PRIEST (1871-1951)

Oscar De Priest was the first African American elected to the United States *House of Representatives* (Congress) in the twentieth century. De Priest was born in Florence, Alabama. He moved to Chicago at the age of eighteen. In Chicago, he worked first as a house painter. Then he went into the real estate business. He became very rich from buying and selling houses. De Priest used this money to launch his career in politics. He was elected as a county commissioner in 1904. In 1915, he was elected as Chicago's first black alderman, serving on the city council. Oscar De Priest was elected to Congress in 1928 as a Republican. He was the first black representative from a Northern state. In Congress, De Priest spoke for all African Americans. He proposed laws that would advance their *civil rights*. He served in Congress until 1932, when he was defeated by a black Democratic candidate named Arthur Mitchell. After leaving Congress, De Priest remained active in Chicago politics. He was elected as an alderman from Chicago's Third Ward in 1943 and served until 1947.

ADAM CLAYTON POWELL, JR. (1908-1972)

Adam Clayton Powell, Jr., grew up in the New York City neighborhood known as Harlem. He was the son of a powerful African American minister. The younger Powell succeeded his father as the pastor of Harlem's Abyssinian Baptist Church in 1937. In addition to being a minister, Powell worked as a community activist and newspaper publisher. He was elected to Congress in 1944. Powell became a leading spokesperson for African Americans while he was in Congress. He sponsored many bills to end racial *discrimination* and *segregation* in programs and institutions that received federal funds. Powell helped convince Congress to pass important social welfare legislation during the 1960's. During that time, Powell was accused of political corruption. He temporarily lost his seat in Congress. The *Supreme Court* then ordered Congress to give him back his position. They ruled that his expulsion from Congress was *unconstitutional*. After being reinstated, Powell served in Congress until 1970, when he was defeated for reelection. In 1971, he retired as pastor of the Abyssinian Baptist Church, and he died in Miami, Florida, in 1972. Powell was known for his ability as a persuasive speaker and for his colorful personality. Many people consider him to be one of the greatest African American politicians.

SHIRLEY CHISHOLM (BORN 1924)

Shirley Chisholm was born in Brooklyn, New York, to parents who had immigrated from the Caribbean island of Barbados. She graduated from Brooklyn College and found a job as a teacher. She was active as a social worker before being elected to the New York state legislature in 1964. In 1968, she was the first African American woman elected to Congress. She was elected to represent the congressional district serving Brooklyn, New York. Chisholm spoke up

An outspoken advocate of minority rights, Shirley Chisholm criticized the Reagan Administration for its cutbacks in social service programs.

about issues that faced African Americans and focused attention on women's issues while she was in Congress. In 1972, she launched her campaign for the Democratic Party nomination for president. Although she did not win the nomination, Chisholm continued to be active in Congress and served on several important committees. After retiring from Congress in 1982, Chisholm taught as a college professor at Mount Holyoke College from 1983 to 1987. In 1993, President Bill Clinton nominated Chisholm to serve as U.S. ambassador to Jamaica.

A NEW GENERATION IN CONGRESS

The careers of Oscar De Priest, Adam Clayton Powell, Jr., and Shirley Chisholm inspired other African Americans to seek election to Congress. Three African American representatives who have served during the 1990's are Carol Moseley Braun, Maxine Waters, and Kweisi Mfume.

CAROL MOSELEY BRAUN (BORN 1947)

Carol Moseley Braun was the first African American woman to be elected to the United States Senate. She grew up in a Catholic family living on Chicago's South Side. Braun earned a law degree in 1972 and worked for a federal prosecutor before she became an attorney. She was elected

to the Illinois state legislature in 1977 and later worked as a recorder of deeds for Cook County. In 1992, she campaigned as a Democratic challenger to represent Illinois in the U.S. Senate. In addition to being the first black woman in the Senate, Braun became only the fourth African American ever to serve in the Senate.

In 1992, Carol Moseley Braun became the first African American woman to be elected to the U.S. Senate.

MAXINE WATERS (BORN 1938)

Maxine Waters was elected to Congress in 1990. Born in St. Louis, Missouri, Waters lived in poverty for many years. She was married at the age of eighteen and moved to California in 1961. After learning about Head Start, an educational program for children of low-income families, Water found work as a teacher and later as a staff supervisor. She eventually became active in local politics in Los Angeles. Waters was first elected to the California state legislature in 1976 and served until 1990. After her election to Congress, she represented one of Los Angeles' African American

Representative Maxine Waters has focused her attention on important social issues that affect the large minority population of her congressional district.

communities in Congress. As a congressional representative, Waters has focused attention on the needs of poor people and minorities in California and elsewhere. She was named as a member of the House Judiciary Committee and was the first nonlawyer to be asked to serve on this influential committee.

KWEISI MFUME (FRIZELL GRAY, BORN 1948)

Kweisi Mfume (pronounced Kwah-EE-see Oom-FOO-may) was elected to Congress in 1986. He was born in Baltimore, Maryland, and taught at a state university before entering politics. Mfume was elected to the Baltimore city council in 1979 and supported the Maryland state activities of the Democratic Party. He also worked as a talk show host before he was elected to Congress in 1986. Like Maxine Waters, he rose out of poverty to become a distinguished congressional representative. During his fourth term in

Congress, Mfume served as the leader of the Congressional Black Caucus, an alliance of black representatives who work together to promote policies and legislation to benefit the African American community.

AFRICAN AMERICAN POLITICS IN THE SOUTH IN THE TWENTIETH CENTURY

Although African Americans made political progress in the North during the twentieth century, they had no political power in the South. They decided to do something about that in the 1960's. African Americans began to challenge the unfair laws that kept them from voting. Organizations such as the *National Association for the Advancement of Colored People (NAACP)* and the *Student Non-Violent Coordinating Committee (SNCC)* tried to register African American voters in Alabama and Mississippi. Groups like the Ku Klux Klan met these efforts with violence. The members of the all-white Ku Klux Klan hated African Americans. They used violence to keep African Americans from voting.

In 1964, hundreds of black and white students came to Mississippi to register African American voters. Local black leaders such as Fannie Lou Hamer also participated in this process. They succeeded in registering many voters but they also came under attack. In June of 1964, three voting rights workers—Andrew Goodman, James Chaney, and Michael Schwerner—were kidnapped and murdered by Ku Klux Klan members. In 1965, the Reverend Martin Luther King, Jr., led hundreds of protesters to Selma, Alabama, to register black voters. Again, they were attacked by members of the Ku Klux Klan and others who did not want African Americans to vote. In response to this violence, President Lyndon B. Johnson persuaded Congress to pass the *Voting Rights Act of 1965*. This law removed all barriers to African American voting in the South. The law also required that federal officials register African Americans to be voters.

This law resulted in millions of African Americans voting in the South. Just as they did after the Civil War,

African Americans elected local sheriffs, judges, state legislators, mayors, and congressional representatives. Many large Southern cities began to elect black mayors, including Atlanta, Georgia; Birmingham, Alabama; New Orleans, Louisiana; and Richmond, Virginia. An African American, Douglas Wilder, was elected the governor of Virginia in 1989.

The Voting Rights Act was renewed in 1982 with new provisions. These provisions resulted in more African Americans going to Congress. By 1993, there were thirty-nine African Americans in Congress. More than half of these representatives were from the South. In 1994, two black incumbents were defeated for reelection, but two new black representatives took seats in the 104th Congress that convened in 1995. The struggle for voting rights in the 1960's made the African American community in the South politically important again. It also helped to free African Americans from a lot of racial discrimination and prejudice. The careers of Douglas Wilder, Andrew Young, and Barbara Jordan are good examples of the strides made by African American politicians in the South.

L. DOUGLAS WILDER (BORN 1931)

Douglas Wilder was born in Richmond, Virginia, in 1931. After graduating from Virginia Union University, he served in the Korean War and was awarded the Bronze Star for his courage. Wilder received his law degree from Howard University and became active with the NAACP Legal Defense Fund. In 1969, he was the first African American to be elected to the Virginia state senate since the Reconstruction era. Although he lost his campaign for a U.S. Senate seat in 1982, he was successful in his campaign to become Virginia's lieutenant governor in 1985. Four years later, Wilder was elected governor of Virginia. He was the first African American to be elected the governor of a state. (In 1872, P. B. S. Pinchback had been appointed to serve as acting governor of Louisiana.) During his term

As U.S. ambassador to the United Nations, Andrew Young (third from lower right) attended many sessions of the U.N. Security Council.

of office, Wilder balanced Virginia's budget without raising taxes. Under Virginia law, Wilder could not run for a second term of office. He left the governor's office in 1993.

ANDREW YOUNG, JR. (BORN 1932)

Andrew Young was born in New Orleans, Louisiana, and moved to Georgia after being ordained as a minister in 1955. He was an active supporter of the Civil Rights movement and worked as a staff member of the *Southern Christian Leadership Conference (SCLC)*. In 1972, Young became the first African American elected to Congress from the South in more than seventy years. He was elected to represent Atlanta in Congress. In 1976, President Jimmy Carter appointed Andrew Young to serve as U.S. ambassador to the United Nations. He served in that position until 1979. In 1981, the voters elected Andrew Young as the mayor of Atlanta. Many new companies brought money and jobs to Atlanta during Young's two terms as mayor. After leaving the mayor's office in 1989, Young campaigned for governor of Georgia in 1990. Although he had lots of support, Young lost in the Democratic primary election. Since then, Young has continued to find ways to serve in community and public affairs. He helped lead the effort to bring the 1996 Summer Olympics to Atlanta.

BARBARA JORDAN (BORN 1936)

Barbara Jordan was the second African American woman to be elected to Congress. She was a champion debater in college and went on to earn her law degree from Boston University in 1959. In 1972, Jordan was elected to represent Texas' Eighteenth Congressional District. She

Undaunted by the symptoms of multiple sclerosis that have confined her to a wheelchair, Barbara Jordan has maintained her leadership status within the Democratic Party.

became famous for her participation on the congressional committee that investigated the Watergate scandal. This investigation eventually caused Richard M. Nixon to step down as president of the United States. During her years in Congress, Jordan also spoke up for civil rights and women's issues. She left Congress in 1978 but remained active within the Democratic Party. She has served as a college professor at the University of Texas and was selected as one of three keynote speakers to address the 1992 Democratic National Convention.

AFRICAN AMERICAN PRESIDENTIAL POLITICS

African American voters have played an important part in twentieth century presidential elections. Their votes helped elect presidents such as Franklin D. Roosevelt in 1944, Harry S Truman in 1948, and John F. Kennedy in 1960. African American voters also helped Jimmy Carter and Bill Clinton become president. In 1972, Shirley Chisholm launched her campaign to seek the presidency. In the 1980's, one notable African American played a major role in presidential politics: Jesse Jackson.

JESSE JACKSON (BORN 1941)

Jesse Jackson is a social activist and political leader who is a hero to millions of African Americans. He was born in Greenville, South Carolina, and won a football scholarship to attend the University of Illinois. Unhappy with his experience there, he transferred to North Carolina Agricultural and Technical State College and helped organize student sit-ins to protest segregation. After graduation, Jackson studied for the ministry. Still concerned with civil rights issues, Jackson began to work full-time for the SCLC as an associate of Martin Luther King, Jr., in 1966. Later, Jackson went out on his own to start Operation PUSH. Operation PUSH was a civil rights and social activist organization located in Chicago. In 1984 and 1988, Jesse Jackson ran for the Democratic Party nomination for president. Although he

In 1988, presidential hopeful Jesse Jackson campaigned for votes from the back of a railroad caboose.

did not win his party's nomination, he did receive many votes. He also created a *"Rainbow Coalition"* to help focus attention on issues facing those Americans who had no political voice. Jackson's strong political showing made him very important to the African American community. During the 1990's, he worked to gain support for making Washington, D.C., the fifty-first state.

Chapter 4

GREAT AFRICAN AMERICAN LEADERS

Although they never held political office, the following African American leaders were very influential. Their activities helped many African American politicians become powerful.

BOOKER T. WASHINGTON (1856-1915)

Booker T. Washington was a well-respected and powerful African American spokesperson and educator. He was born a slave in Virginia and received his freedom after the Civil War ended. Washington wanted an education so much that he walked across the state of Virginia to attend Hampton Institute, a school founded in 1868 to educated freed slaves. After he graduated from Hampton Institute, Washington established a similar school in Alabama called the Tuskegee Institute. This school became the most important college for African Americans in this country. Tuskegee Institute trained African Americans to be carpenters, bricklayers, shoemakers, and other skilled workers. In a famous speech he gave in 1896, Washington called for African Americans to work together with white Americans to create a new and prosperous South. This speech made him very popular and powerful. Until his death in 1915, Booker T. Washington was the most

Booker T. Washington promoted education as a means of advancement for African Americans.

powerful African American in the United States. He used that power to shape the education of African Americans and to build up black businesses and farms.

W. E. B. Du Bois (1868-1963)

W. E. B. Du Bois was an important African American thinker, writer, and teacher. He was born in Massachusetts and was educated at Fisk and Harvard universities. He became a college professor at Atlanta University. During his time in Atlanta, Du Bois wrote *The Souls of Black Folk* (1903). This important book criticized Booker T. Washington for his failure to speak out against racial discrimination in the South. Du Bois also criticized Washington for saying that African

Americans should work with their hands and not their minds. Du Bois believed that African Americans needed to be educated to be doctors, lawyers, teachers, and political leaders, as well as to be skilled workers. In 1909, Du Bois helped start the National Association for the Advancement of Colored People (NAACP). He stayed with them for many years. He was the editor of their magazine *The Crisis*. He wrote many other books and magazine articles that called for the freedom of African Americans from racial oppression. He was persecuted by the government for his criticism of racism. Because of this *persecution*, W. E. B. Du Bois moved to the African country of Ghana. He died in Ghana at the age of ninety-five in 1963.

MARCUS GARVEY (1887-1941)

Marcus Garvey was born in Jamaica in 1887. He moved to the United States in 1916. Garvey was famous for his dream of an Africa free from European control. In 1917, he formed the Universal Negro Improvement Association (UNIA) to make this dream come true. This organization established businesses, schools, a newspaper, and a church in New York and other parts of the country. Garvey spread his message that African Americans were descendants of a proud and mighty people who at one time controlled the African continent. He wanted African Americans to return to Africa to free it from outside control. His message was very popular with African Americans. By the early 1920's, the UNIA was the most powerful organization in the black community. Unfortunately, the UNIA ran into financial problems. The U.S. government began looking for evidence to use to send Garvey back to Jamaica. In 1923, Garvey was charged with mail fraud and was sent to prison in 1925. After he was released from prison in 1927, he was sent back to Jamaica. For the rest of his life, Garvey tried to restart the UNIA and continued to convince others to help free Africa from European control. He died in London in 1940. Sadly, Marcus Garvey never got the chance to visit Africa himself.

MARY MCLEOD BETHUNE (1875-1955)

Mary McLeod Bethune was a great African American educator. In 1904, she founded a school in Daytona Beach, Florida, that eventually became Bethune-Cookman College. She watched it grow from a small one-room school to a large, well-endowed institution. She also was a spokesperson for African American women's issues and helped to start the National Council for Negro Women. During the 1930's, Bethune was in charge of African American youth programs for the federal government.

THURGOOD MARSHALL (1908-1993)

Thurgood Marshall was a great African American lawyer and judge. He was the leader of the NAACP's team of lawyers for many years. In the famous case of *Brown v. Board of Education* in 1954, he convinced the Supreme Court to declare racial segregation in public education unconstitutional. In 1967, President Lyndon B. Johnson appointed Thurgood Marshall as the first African American member of the Supreme Court. While on the Supreme Court, Marshall was a strong defender of the constitutional rights of African Americans, other minorities, and the poor.

As a young lawyer with the NAACP, Thurgood Marshall argued the case of **Brown v. Board of Education** *before the Supreme Court in 1954.*

Martin Luther King, Jr., addresses the huge crowds who participated in the historic 1963 March on Washington.

MARTIN LUTHER KING, JR. (1929-1968)

Martin Luther King, Jr., was one of the greatest African Americans of all time. He was born in Atlanta, Georgia. His father was a minister at Ebenezer Baptist Church in Atlanta. After graduating from Morehouse College, the younger King decided to become a minister as well. He received a doctoral degree in theology from Boston University in 1951. After finishing his degree, King became a pastor of a church in Montgomery, Alabama. While living in Montgomery, King led a successful effort to end racial segregation on that city's public buses. This effort, called the Montgomery Bus Boycott, made King very famous. Later, he started the Southern Christian Leadership Conference (SCLC), which led civil rights protests all over the South.

Soon King became the leading spokesperson for the freedom struggle of African Americans. In 1963, he led the March on Washington and gave his famous "I Have a Dream" speech at the foot of the Lincoln Memorial. In his speech, King called for a nation in which racial discrimination and oppression did not exist. King led many other civil rights marches and demonstrations that pressured Congress into passing the *Civil Rights Act of 1964* and the Voting Rights Act of 1965. These laws allowed African Americans to shop, travel, and vote freely in the South. In the late 1960's, King spoke out against the Vietnam War. He also spoke up for ending poverty in the United States. He was planning a Poor People's March on Washington, D.C., when he was killed in Memphis, Tennessee, in 1968 by a white racist named James Earl Ray. To honor King and his accomplishments, his birthday was made a national holiday in 1982.

MALCOLM X (1925-1965)

Malcolm X was one of the greatest African American leaders of all time. He was born Malcolm Little in Omaha, Nebraska, in 1925. After his father died in mysterious circumstances, Malcolm's family broke up. Malcolm was eventually sent to Boston to live with his sister. While living in Boston and in New York, he became a small-time criminal. He was sent to prison for burglary. During his time in prison, Malcolm turned his life around. He spent his time reading books and educating himself. He discovered the religious teachings of the *Nation of Islam* and became a member.

When he was released from prison, Malcolm became a minister in the Nation of Islam. He changed his name from "Little" to "X" to show his rejection of a "slave" name. Malcolm X traveled around the country establishing Muslim temples. He spread the word of Elijah Muhammad. Malcolm became famous for his criticism of racial oppression. He expressed the anger that many African Americans felt over their status within the United States. He called for African Americans to be proud of themselves and their past. He wanted African Americans to love and respect each other. He also wanted them to fight racist oppression wherever it was.

Malcolm X left the Nation of Islam to form his own Muslim organization in 1964. He also traveled to Mecca, the Muslim holy city in Saudi Arabia. Malcolm X's message challenged many people's assumptions about African Americans. He had a lot of enemies. In February of 1965, Malcolm X was murdered while giving a speech in New York City. Although he died, his message of African American self-respect and pride and his struggle against racism did not die. He is still revered and respected by African Americans today.

The image of Malcolm X on this man's jacket pays tribute to Malcolm's fearless attacks on racism.

NOTABLE AFRICAN AMERICAN POLITICIANS

United States Senate

	Years	Party	State
Hiram R. Revels	1870-1871	Republican	Mississippi
Blanche K. Bruce	1875-1881	Republican	Mississippi
Edward W. Brooke	1967-1979	Republican	Massachusetts
Carol Moseley Braun	1993-	Democratic	Illinois

United States House of Representatives

	Years	Party	State
Joseph H. Rainey	1870-1879	Republican	South Carolina
Jefferson F. Long	1870-1871	Republican	Georgia
Robert B. Elliott	1871-1874	Republican	South Carolina
Robert C. De Large	1871-1873	Republican	South Carolina
Benjamin S. Turner	1871-1873	Republican	Alabama
Josiah T. Walls	1871-1873, 1873-1876	Republican	Florida
Richard H. Cain	1873-1875, 1877-1879	Republican	South Carolina
John R. Lynch	1873-1877, 1882-1883	Republican	Mississippi
James T. Rapier	1873-1875	Republican	Alabama
Alonzo J. Ransier	1873-1875	Republican	South Carolina
Jeremiah Haralson	1875-1877	Republican	Alabama
John A. Hyman	1875-1877	Republican	North Carolina
Charles E. Nash	1875-1877	Republican	Louisiana
Robert Smalls	1875-1879, 1882-1883, 1884-1887	Republican	South Carolina
James E. O'Hara	1883-1887	Republican	North Carolina
Henry P. Cheatham	1889-1893	Republican	North Carolina
John M. Langston	1890-1891	Republican	Virginia
Thomas E. Miller	1890-1891	Republican	South Carolina
George W. Murray	1893-1895, 1896-1897	Republican	South Carolina

	Years	Party	State
George H. White	1897-1901	Republican	North Carolina
Oscar De Priest	1929-1935	Republican	Illinois
Arthur W. Mitchell	1935-1943	Democratic	Illinois
William L. Dawson	1943-1970	Democratic	Illinois
Adam Clayton Powell, Jr.	1945-1967, 1969-1971	Democratic	New York
Charles C. Diggs, Jr.	1955-1980	Democratic	Michigan
Robert N. C. Nix, Sr.	1958-1978	Democratic	Pennsylvania
Augustus F. Hawkins	1963-1990	Democratic	California
John Conyers, Jr.	1965-	Democratic	Michigan
William L. Clay	1969-	Democratic	Missouri
Louis Stokes	1969-	Democratic	Ohio
Shirley Chisholm	1969-1983	Democratic	New York
George W. Collins	1970-1972	Democratic	Illinois
Ronald V. Dellums	1971-	Democratic	California
Walter E. Fauntroy	1971-1991	Democratic	Washington, D.C.
Ralph H. Metcalfe	1971-1978	Democratic	Illinois
Parren J. Mitchell	1971-1987	Democratic	Maryland
Charles B. Rangel	1971-	Democratic	New York
Yvonne Brathwaite Burke	1973-1979	Democratic	California
Cardiss Collins	1973-	Democratic	Illinois
Barbara C. Jordan	1973-1979	Democratic	Texas
Andrew J. Young	1973-1977	Democratic	Georgia
Harold E. Ford	1975-	Democratic	Tennessee
Julian C. Dixon	1979-	Democratic	California
Melvin H. Evans	1979-1981	Republican	Virgin Islands
William H. Gray III	1979-1991	Democratic	Pennsylvania
George "Mickey" Leland	1979-1989	Democratic	Texas
Bennett Stewart	1979-1981	Democratic	Illinois
George W. Crockett, Jr.	1980-1991	Democratic	Michigan
Mervyn M. Dymally	1981-1993	Democratic	California
Augustus F. "Gus" Savage	1981-1993	Democratic	Illinois
Harold Washington	1981-1983	Democratic	Illinois
Katie Hall	1982-1985	Democratic	Indiana
Charles Hayes	1983-1993	Democratic	Illinois

	Years	*Party*	*State*
Major R. Owens	1983-	Democratic	New York
Edolphus Towns	1983-	Democratic	New York
Alan D. Wheat	1983-	Democratic	Missouri
Alton R. Waldon, Jr.	1986-1987	Democratic	New York
Michael Espy	1987-1992	Democratic	Mississippi
Floyd H. Flake	1987-	Democratic	New York
John Lewis	1987-	Democratic	Georgia
Kweisi Mfume	1987-	Democratic	Maryland
Donald M. Payne	1989-	Democratic	New Jersey
Craig Washington	1990-1995	Democratic	Texas
Lucien E. Blackwell	1991-1995	Democratic	Pennsylvania
Barbara-Rose Collins	1991-	Democratic	Michigan
Gary A. Franks	1991-	Republican	Connecticut
William J. Jefferson	1991-	Democratic	Louisiana
Eleanor Holmes Norton	1991-	Democratic	Washington, D.C.
Maxine Waters	1991-	Democratic	California
Sanford Bishop	1993-	Democratic	Georgia
Corinne Brown	1993-	Democratic	Florida
Eva M. Clayton	1993-	Democratic	North Carolina
James E. Clyburn	1993-	Democratic	South Carolina
Cleo Fields	1993-	Democratic	Louisiana
Alcee L. Hastings	1993-	Democratic	Florida
Earl F. Hilliard	1993-	Democratic	Alabama
Eddie Bernice Johnson	1993-	Democratic	Texas
Cynthia McKinney	1993-	Democratic	Georgia
Carrie P. Meek	1993-	Democratic	Florida
Mel Reynolds	1993-	Democratic	Illinois
Bobby L. Rush	1993-	Democratic	Illinois
Robert C. "Bobby" Scott	1993-	Democratic	Virginia
Bennie G. Thompson	1993-	Democratic	Mississippi
Walter R. Tucker	1993-	Democratic	California
Melvin Watt	1993-	Democratic	North Carolina
Albert R. Wynn	1993-	Democratic	Maryland
Sheila Jackson Lee	1995-	Democratic	Texas
J. C. Watts	1995-	Republican	Oklahoma

GLOSSARY

civil rights: The legal rights people enjoy as citizens of a nation, such as the right to vote, the right to free speech, and the right to privacy.

Civil Rights Act of 1964: A law that declared racial segregation and discrimination in public places to be illegal. Black people were given equal access to restaurants, theaters, hotels and motels, railroads, buses, airplanes, and airports previously denied to them.

Congress: The legislature of the United States, which is responsible for making the laws of the nation. This legislature is composed of two bodies, the House of Representatives and the Senate.

discrimination: Unfair treatment of an individual or a group because of their skin color or ethnic heritage.

House of Representatives: One of the two bodies of the U.S. Congress, consisting of people elected to represent all the local areas of the United States.

Kemet: Another name for ancient Egypt.

legislation: A law passed by elected politicians in local, state, or federal government.

ma'at: Principles that guided the people of Egypt and other African civilizations. These principles included truth, justice, righteousness, harmony, fairness, balance, and order.

Nation of Islam: An important African American religious, political, and social group. It began around 1930 as the Black Muslims, founded by W. D. Fard, and was taken over in late 1933 or early 1934 by Elijah Muhammad. Muhammad preached black separatism: He said that African Americans must create a strong, positive image of themselves and live independently from oppressive white society. Malcolm X became a leader of this group in the 1950's but was assassinated in 1965. After Elijah Muhammad died in 1975, the group's leadership eventually passed to Louis Farrakhan.

National Association for the Advancement of Colored People (NAACP): An organization founded in 1909 by both black and white socialists to protest Jim Crow and other discriminatory laws. Over the years, the NAACP became one of the key organizations working for African American rights and made great advances. In recent years, its existence has been threatened by controversy over the competency of some leaders.

persecution: Mistreating or harassing someone because of his or her beliefs.

politics: The organized activities surrounding efforts to govern any group or community of people (such as a nation), especially those activities concerned with getting and maintaining positions of power and leadership. Such activities are usually connected with campaigns for elected office in civil governments, but politics may also be connected with churches and other organizations.

poll tax: A fee, or amount of cash, that used to be required before a person could vote. Poll taxes were often used to keep poor African Americans from exercising their right to vote.

Rainbow Coalition: A term used by Jesse Jackson during his campaigns for the U.S. presidency in 1984 and 1988 to refer to his supporters. The term "rainbow" referred to the many different races and ethnicities of the people who supported Jackson.

segregation: Laws or customs that forced black people and white people to keep apart. These practices kept African Americans out of public places, schools, and neighborhoods.

Senate: The body of the U.S. Congress that consists of one hundred members called senators. Two senators from each state are elected by that state's citizens to represent the state in Congress.

slavery: The system of ownership of human beings for the purpose of forced labor.

Southern Christian Leadership Conference (SCLC): Formed in 1957, this organization advanced the Civil Rights movement that was forming in the South and had members such as Martin Luther King, Jr., Ralph Abernathy, Jr., Andrew Young, and Jesse Jackson. It worked to desegregate public facilities and increase voter participation. The group continues to work to increase economic opportunities for African Americans.

Student Non-Violent Coordinating Committee (SNCC): A student organization active during the Civil Rights movement of the 1960's. The SNCC coordinated the political activities of students involved in African American causes, such as protest rallies and voter registration.

Supreme Court: The highest court in the United States. It rules on the laws of the land and how they are to be interpreted. Many cases that have come before the

Supreme Court have determined changes in American society; in *Brown v. Board of Education* (1954), for example, the Court overturned an earlier ruling that "separate but equal" facilities did not violate African Americans' rights.

Thirteenth Amendment:
This amendment to the U.S. Constitution reads in part, "Neither slavery nor involuntary servitude . . . shall exist within the United States, or any place subject to their jurisdiction."

unconstitutional: Laws or practices not allowed by the United States Constitution, the highest law of the land. The Supreme Court is the highest legal body that can decide whether or not a law or practice is constitutional.

Voting Rights Act of 1965: This law removed unfair barriers that prevented African Americans from voting in the South. After the act was passed, many African Americans were elected as representatives in local, state, and federal government.

MORE ABOUT AFRICAN AMERICANS AND POLITICS

Albert, Peter J., and Ronald Hoffman, eds. *We Shall Overcome: Martin Luther King and the Black Freedom Struggle.* New York: Pantheon Books, 1990.

Brownmiller, Susan. *Shirley Chisholm: A Biography.* Garden City, N.Y.: Doubleday, 1971.

Clay, William L. *Just Permanent Interests: Black Americans in Congress, 1870-1991.* New York: Amistad Press, 1992.

Franklin, John Hope, and Alfred A. Moss, Jr. *From Slavery to Freedom: A History of African Americans.* 7th ed. New York: McGraw-Hill, 1994.

Harding, Vincent. *There Is a River: The Black Struggle for Freedom in America.* 2d ed. New York: Harcourt Brace Jovanovich, 1993.

Haskins, James. *Adam Clayton Powell: Portrait of a Marching Black.* New York: Dial Press, 1974.

_____. *Picture Life of Malcolm X.* New York: Franklin Watts, 1975.

Miller, Alton. *Harold Washington: The Mayor, the Man.* Chicago: Bonus Books, 1989.

Rubel, David. *Fannie Lou Hamer: From Sharecropping to Politics.* Englewood Cliffs, N.J.: Silver Burdett Press, 1990.

INDEX